LUXURY BATHROOMS

JAMES GRAYSON TRULOVE

LUXURY BATHROOMS

JAMES GRAYSON TRULOVE

COLLINS | **DESIGN**

An Imprint of HarperCollinsPublishers

HarperCollins books may be purchased for educational, business, or sales promotional use.
For information, please write: Special Markets Department, HarperCollins*Publishers*,
10 East 53rd Street, New York, NY 10022.

First published in 2008 by:
Collins Design
An Imprint of HarperCollins*Publishers*
10 East 53rd Street
New York, NY 10022
Tel: (212) 207-7000
Fax: (212) 207-7654
collinsdesign@harpercollins.com
www.harpercollins.com

Distributed throughout the world by:
HarperCollins*Publishers*
10 East 53rd Street
New York, NY 10022
Fax: (212) 207-7654

Packaged by:
Grayson Publishing, LLC
James G. Trulove, Publisher
1250 28th Street NW
Washington, DC 20007
(202) 337-1380
jtrulove@aol.com

Designed by: Agnieszka Stachowicz

Library of Congress Control Number: 2007933891
ISBN: 978-0-06-134828-0

Printed in China
First printing, 2008

CONTENTS

Spa-like luxury bathrooms—the kind usually associated with four-star resorts—are making their way into American homes. A recent front-page report in *The New York Times* proclaimed that more money is being spent on renovating the bathroom that any other part of the home, including the kitchen. The popularity of resort travel along with the increased emphasis on fitness and general well-being have fueled this interest in turning the bathroom—or home spa—into a major destination within the home, right up there with the kitchen.

Architects, designers, and manufactures are responding by offering a wide range of options for creating and outfitting the bathroom. From oversized stone bathtubs with faucets that resemble cascading waterfalls to steam rooms, saunas and "smart toilets," a properly out-fitted bathroom can now cost the same as a a luxury automobile. But unlike the car, a luxury bathroom can add value to the home when it is time to sell.

This book presents the latest in innovative luxury bathroom design by architects from across the country, featuring a range of bathroom designs in a variety of settings from vacation homes to primary residences and apartments, from rustic cabins such as those designed by the Seattle, Washington architectural firm, Balance Associates to ultra-sophisticated bathroom creations by the New York firm Hanrahan and Meyers. In several cases, multiple bathrooms by the same architect are presented to illustrate how one architect or firm addresses the needs of wildly diverse clients.

To help the reader better understand how these bathrooms are configured and how they relate to the other rooms in the home, floor plans are presented for each of the bathrooms, making it easier for the reader to plan similar spaces for their own bathrooms and take advantage of luxury bathroom mania that is sweeping the country!

FOREWORD

A GENTLEMAN'S BATHROOM

ARCHITECT Christian Zapatka Architect

PHOTOGRAPHY Bob Narod

Conceived of as a classic washroom in an early twentieth-century men's club, this bathroom features a palette of mahogany, mirror and marble. The space is achieved by combining what had previously been a small dressing room and a pink-tiled bathroom original to the 1959 wing of a large townhouse. The long but relatively narrow proportions of the renovated space are made more pleasing by anchoring the ends of the rooms with "cabinets," one for a steam shower clad in slabs of book-matched statuary marble and the other for a water closet delineated by a screen of mahogany panels, one with a frosted glass panel that serves as the door. Mirrored glass panels in the upper portions of this "cabinet" visually widen the space.

The central area is reserved for a high double vanity in mahogany topped by a honed Nero Marquina slab and a shallow floor-to-ceiling mahogany dressing cabinet with a Nero Marquina slab and a mirrored glass panel at a height convenient for tying neckties. The two full-size windows flanking this cabinet are screened from the street below by mahogany blinds. Operable panels in both mahogany and mirrored glass above the vanity conceal shallow shelving. The polished nickel faucets in this bathroom are from the Aero line at Waterworks.

PRINCIPAL MATERIALS PALETTE
- STATUARY MARBLE
- MAHOGANY PANELS
- HONED NERO MARQUINA SLAB
- POLISHED NICKEL
- MIRRORED GLASS

LEFT: The double vanity and the
floor-to-ceiling cabinetry are constructed of mahogany to give the
feeling of a gentleman's clubroom.

RIGHT: The shallow floor-to-ceiling
mahogany dressing cabinet has a
Nero Marquina slab top. The mirror
is positioned at a height convenient
for tying neckties.

FLOOR PLAN

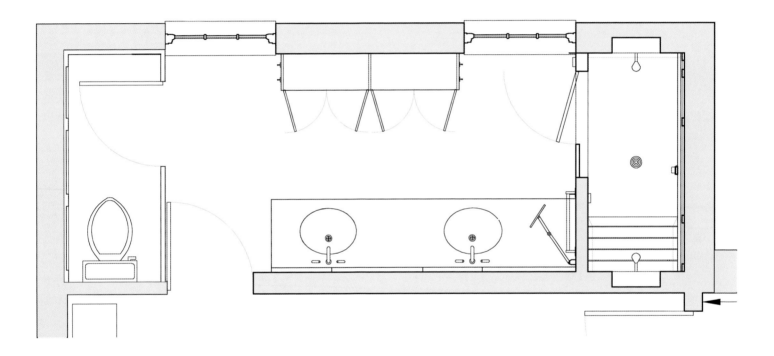

TWO BATHROOMS IN ONE

ARCHITECT Christian Zapatka Architect

PHOTOGRAPHY Christopher Campbell

One big bathroom or two smaller ones within the same space—these were the options for this project in a railroad-type apartment. Ultimately, a pair of cramped back-to-back existing bathrooms in the middle of the apartment were removed and replaced with a big curving room that borrows an arc of space from an unusually wide side hall. The finished space is normally used as a single, spalike bathroom with an extra-long stainless steel tub positioned along the curved wall, a centrally placed shower, and separate vanities and toilets at each end of the room.

When two bathrooms are needed, sand-blasted glass panels can be slid out from the sides of the shower along ceiling tracks and hook into the curved outer wall to create two private areas. Depending on whether one or both of the panels is pulled, the resulting options are one bathroom with both tub and shower, plus a separate powder room; or two bathrooms, one with a tub and one with a shower.

The curved wall projecting into the hall is tiled with sea-green glass mosaic on the inside and red-painted wallboard on the outside, alternating with double-sided frosted glass light boxes. The interior walls of the bathroom combine the same glass mosaic tile with panels of stained birch plywood and mirrored glass. The low ceilings are covered in stained plywood, lending a saunalike atmosphere. The vanity countertops are polished, poured-in-place concrete slabs.

PRINCIPAL MATERIALS PALETTE
- GLASS MOSAIC
- FROSTED GLASS
- STAINED BIRCH PLYWOOD
- STAINLESS STEEL
- MIRRORED GLASS
- POURED-IN-PLACE CONCRETE SLAB

PREVIOUS PAGES: A view of the shower and the stainless steel tub with the frosted panels in the open position. When the panels are closed, the single bathroom becomes two, one with a tub and the other with a shower.

PREVIOUSLY EXISTING FLOOR PLAN

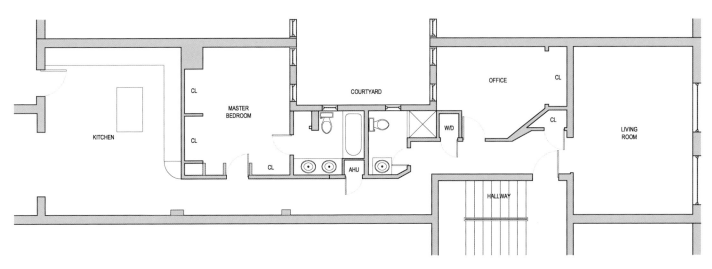

AS-BUILT FLOOR PLAN

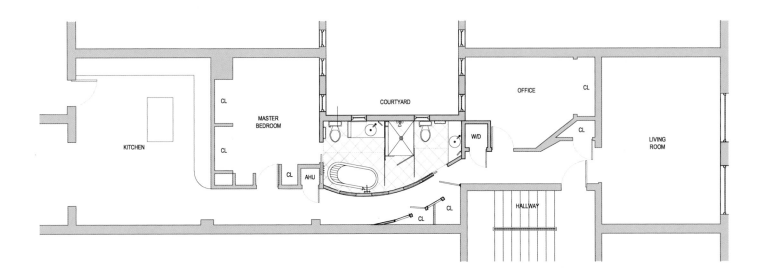

AS-BUILT FLOOR PLAN

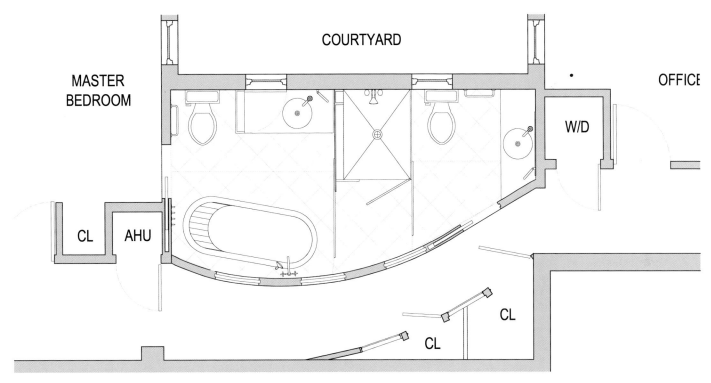

COURTYARD

MASTER
BEDROOM

OFFICE

W/D

CL   AHU

CL

CL

SOUTH ELEVATION

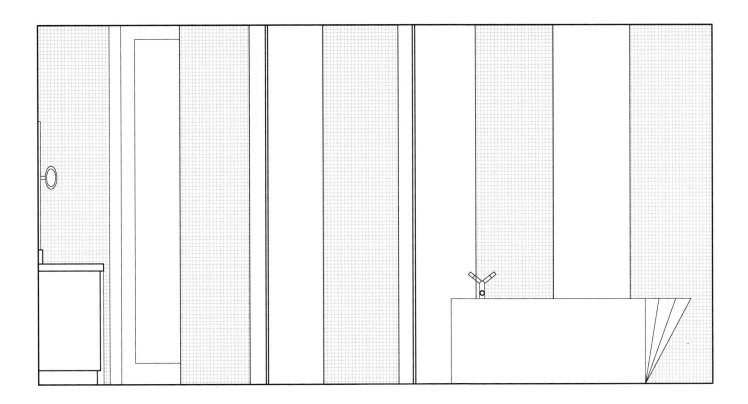

LEFT: The curved wall with its glass mosaic tile and translucent frosted glass panels provides added width to the narrow space. The view is from the tub half of the bathroom, looking past the movable glass panels to the shower half. The ceilings are sheathed in stained plywood to give a saunalike feel to the bathroom.

NORTH ELEVATION

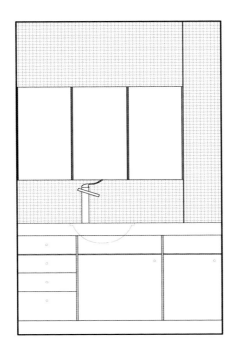

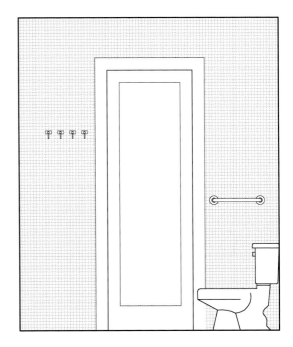

WEST/EAST ELEVATION

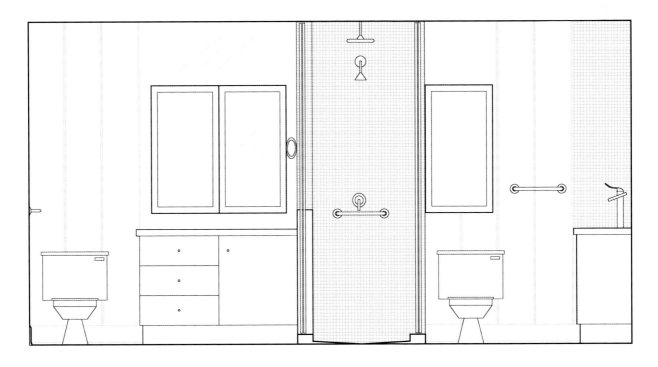

LEFT: Frosted glass panels over the vanity bring in natural light from an adjacent courtyard. This is a view from the shower side of the bathroom looking toward the stainless steel tub side.

AWASH IN MARBLE

ARCHITECT Christian Zapatka Architect

PHOTOGRAPHY Homevisit.com

The master bathroom in this large, historic townhouse occupies 300 square feet at the end of the master bedroom wing of the house. It features a double shower with multiple sources of water, a plunge-pool-size whirlpool bathtub, two vanities, two separate water closets, and, to complete the spa-like experience, a coffee bar around the corner.

The walls are lined from floor to ceiling in a running band pattern of Calacatta marble punctuated by narrow bands of gray-green limestone. The floor is covered with the same combination of stone in a mosaic scale rug pattern. Natural light is admitted to the room through a pair of windows facing the street to the west and a pair of windows facing a park-size garden to the east as well as a skylight capturing overhead light. Artificial light is provided by three alabaster urn-type lamps suspended by polished nickel chains from the ceiling, alabaster wall sconces in the water closets, and two groupings of recessed ceiling lamps that highlight the colors and patterns of the stone walls and floor. Custom-designed mirrors over the vanities are lit by low-voltage tube lamps filtered by frosted glass panels in the depth of the surrounding ebony-stained wood box frames. The vanity cabinets are crafted of the same ebony-stained wood, and all faucets are polished nickel from the Aero line at Waterworks.

PRINCIPAL MATERIALS PALETTE
- CALACATTA MARBLE
- FROSTED GLASS
- LIMESTONE
- ALABASTER
- MIRRORED GLASS
- EBONY-STAINED WOOD

EXISTING MASTER BEDROOM/BATH FLOOR PLAN

PREVIOUS PAGES: This generously proportioned bathroom has adjacent glass-walled showers and a long, deep soaking tub. The walls are covered in Calacattta marble with narrow bands of gray-green lime-stone tiles.

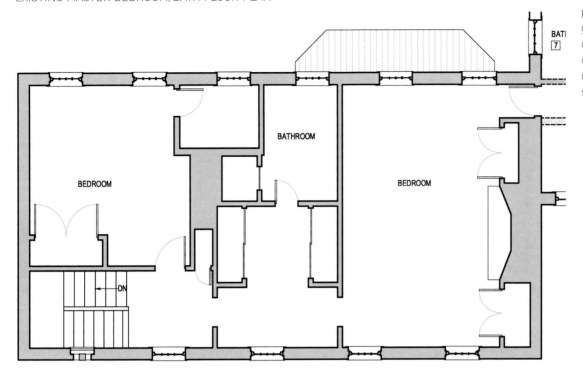

AS-BUILT MASTER BEDROOM/BATH PLAN

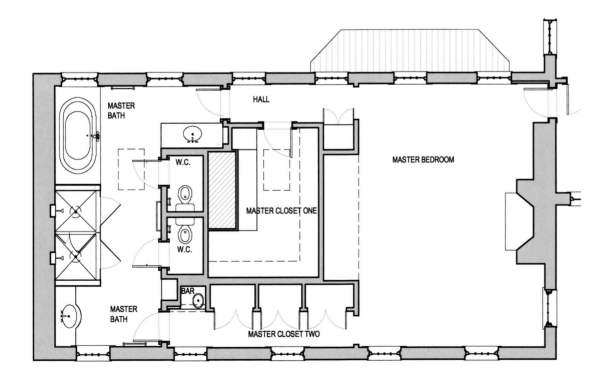

MASTER BATH VANITY/SHOWER ELEVATION

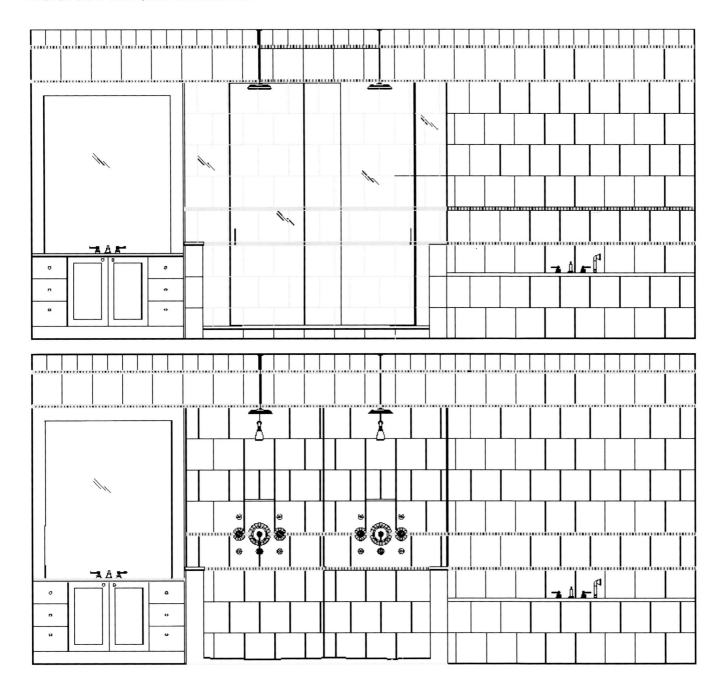

LEFT: A view of the ebony-stained wooden vanity adjacent to the glass-enclosed double showers.
FOLLOWING PAGES: A window over the second vanity provides soothing views into the garden of the townhouse.

MASTER BATH ELEVATIONS

MASTER BATH WATER CLOSET ELEVATIONS

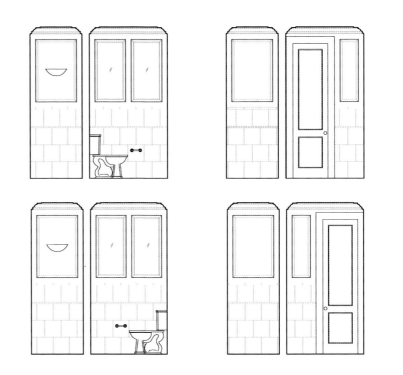

A STONE LANDSCAPE

ARCHITECT Christian Zapatka Architect

PHOTOGRAPHY Christopher Campbell

Carved out of a warren of corridors, closets, and a hall bathroom, this new bathroom is nearly a cube whose outer dimension is twelve feet. Daylight is admitted to the space by a four-foot-diameter oculus enclosed within a stainless steel and plaster canopy that appears to be floating in space. Suspended by steel chains from the rafters, the canopy conceals a six-foot-square skylight. At night, artificial light sources tucked between the ceiling and the canopy make the surrounding plaster appear translucent.

Three of the walls of the room are lined in a grid of panels veneered in pearwood and outlined in stainless steel banding. Two panels serve as doors to the room, and a third opens into the water closet. A clear glass panel screens the shower stall, while mirrored glass and pearwood panels adorn the opposite wall.

The focal point of the room provided by a pair of monumental, book-matched slabs of Indian picture stone—their ragged edges still exposed—offers a landscapelike backdrop to a pair of back-to-back clear glass washstands. The wall is up-lit by a series of lights embedded in the river-pebble-paved floor. Separating the washstands is a two-sided mirror that is integrally lit and framed in a stainless steel bracket suspended from the ceiling, and below, a pearwood-paneled box conceals the plumbing lines and electric outlets and switches.

PRINCIPAL MATERIALS PALETTE

- INDIAN PICTURE STONE
- CLEAR GLASS
- PEARWOOD
- STAINLESS STEEL
- MIRRORED GLASS
- RIVER PEBBLES

PREVIOUSLY EXISTING THIRD FLOOR PLAN

PREVIOUS PAGES: Flanked by
pearwood paneling, the Indian
picture stone provides a dramatic
backdrop for the twin washbasins.
Uplighting embedded in the river-
pebble floor enhances the drama
of the wall.

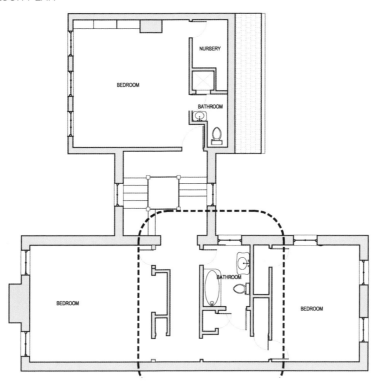

BEDROOM

NURSERY

BATHROOM

BEDROOM

BATHROOM

BEDROOM

AS-BUILT THIRD FLOOR PLAN

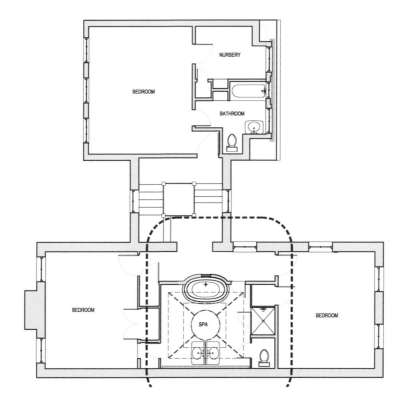

BEDROOM

NURSERY

BATHROOM

BEDROOM

SPA

BEDROOM

SPA PLAN

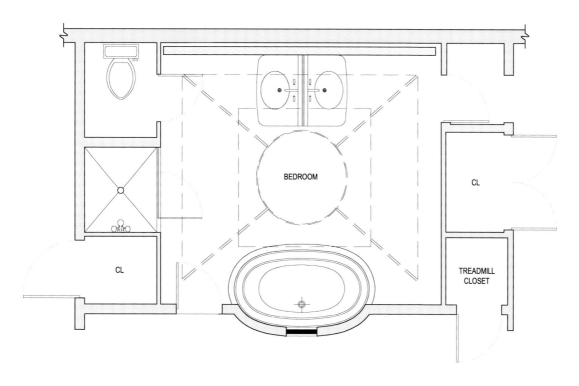

EAST-WEST SPA ELEVATION

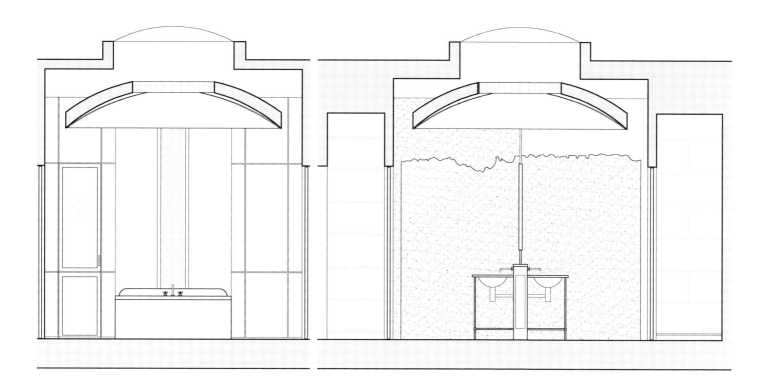

LEFT: A view of the washbasins with natural lighting provided by the four-foot oculus.

ABOVE: A black whirlpool tub is encased in pearwood. A ribbed black granite slab is washed with a steady sheet of water from a concealed source overhead.

FOLLOWING PAGES: The oculus appears to float from the ceiling when viewed from below.

DAYLIGHT-FILLED BATHROOMS

ARCHITECT Mark Simon with Meg Lyons, Centerbrook Architects and Planners

PHOTOGRAPHY Peter Aaron/Esto Photographics

This house faces the Long Island Sound to the south across a rolling lawn. The clients wanted a house filled with daylight and tied closely to the landscape around it.

The powder room on the first floor was made larger than usual and includes a shower. This allows it to double as a wheelchair-accessible bathroom if our owners should find it necessary to live entirely on the first floor of the house. A half-round bay of windows above the sink counter brings in ample natural light.

Upstairs, the master bedroom suite is ringed with windows offering water views. The bathroom has windows set high on the north wall to provide light but preserve privacy without the need for shutters. A brindle mix of brown, pink, and gray granite is used on the sink and on the walls of the walk-in shower. The floor is dark natural cleft slate tiles. Two closets are provided for linen and toiletry storage. The shower has a bench, and a skylight keeps the shower light and airy.

PRINCIPAL MATERIALS PALETTE
- BLUE BANIA GRANITE
- NATURAL CLEFT SLATE TILES
- MAPLE
- GLAZED BLUE TILES
- MIX OF BROWN, PINK, AND GREY GRANITE

FIRST FLOOR POWDER ROOM

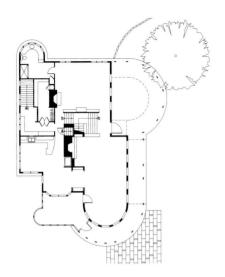

SECOND FLOOR MASTER BATHROOM

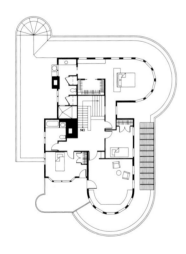

PREVIOUS PAGES: On the first floor, a large powder room with a shower has a bay of windows above the sink counter.

RIGHT AND FAR RIGHT: The master bathroom benefits from ample natural light streaming through windows as well as a large skylight over the granite-encased shower.

OPENNESS AND LIGHT

ARCHITECT Mark Simon, Centerbrook Architects and Planners

PHOTOGRAPHY Albert Vecerka/Esto Photographics

This house for a pair of empty nesters rose from the ashes of their earlier home, the victim of an electrical fire. The owners wanted plentiful daylight but needed to limit summer heat from direct light. They desired a clean, modern aesthetic. The house has a gable roof with large overhangs, allowing substantial floor-to-ceiling glass for views and indirect daylight. Light and a sense of openness fill the house.

The master bedroom has a cathedral ceiling to bounce light about. The master bath is tiled in slate, with a tub standing free in the room, next to an open shower. The slate is uniformally the same, however it is laid in different sizes for function and for a variety of texture.

The powder room on the first floor is tiled in multicolored slate and has a strip of narrow frosted windows to let in daylight from the entry hall.

PRINCIPAL MATERIALS PALETTE
- SLATE
- MIRROWED GLASS
- STAINLESS STEEL

FIRST FLOOR POWDER ROOM

PREVIOUS PAGES: The master
bathroom is tiled in slate from the
vanity area to the walk-in shower.
RIGHT: The free-standing bathtub is
visible in the mirror of the vanity.
FOLLOWING PAGES: Frosted glass
openings in the wall of the power
room allow natural light to filter into
the space. The walls are covered
with multicolored slate tiles.

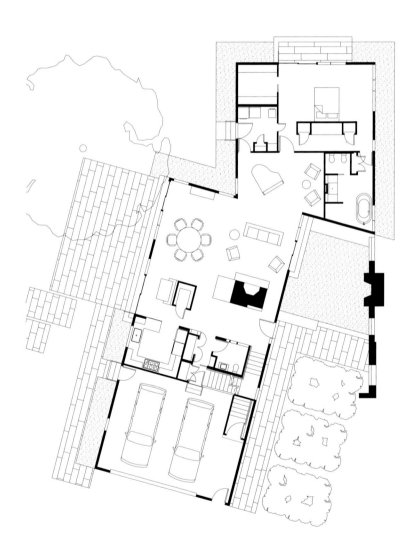

A RICH PALETTE

ARCHITECT HanrahanMeyers Architects

PHOTOGRAPHY Michael Moran

This large, 5,000-square-foot apartment consists of a master bedroom, two guest bedrooms, and three and one-half baths. The architects designed the apartment with a rich and varied palette of cherry and ash wood; stainless steel; glass; roughened, unfinished slate tiles; and honed limestone slabs for counters. This palette is reflected in the overall design of the bathrooms as well.

Near the center of the apartment in the entrance area is a cube made of cherry that is wrapped with bookcases and encloses a bathroom. The sand-blasted glass entry door leads to a warm and inviting space where the counters and tub enclosure are made of honed limestone. The walls are cherry panels and glass mosaic tile. All bathroom floors in the apartment are heated beneath roughened slate tiles.

The master bath features a whirlpool tub with a honed limestone enclosure. The tub is flanked by a glass shower with limestone mosaic floor tiles. There are sink areas on both sides of the master bath. On one side, the sink is positioned in front of a window that has sandblasted glass for privacy. A hinged mirror can be centered above the sink or set to the side. The sink's ash cabinet continues to the floor and can be used for extra towels or other items.

The powder room is lined with cherry, mirror, glass, and stainless steel. A white porcelain sink by is mounted on a custom cherry washstand.

The overall intention in the design of all four baths was to establish an organic sensibility through the use of natural materials. The ceramic tiles used are handmade with a clear glaze on a naturally cream-colored fired clay.

PRINCIPAL MATERIALS PALETTE

- ASH AND CHERRY WOOD
- SAND-BLASTED GLASS
- SLATE
- LIMESTONE
- STAINLESS STEEL

FLOOR PLAN

PREVIOUS PAGES: A view of the floating cherry cube that encloses one of the four bathrooms in the apartment. The sand-blasted door provides privacy while admiting light into the windowless space. FOLLOWING PAGES: The palette of rich material is employed in the design of each of the four bathrooms. One great luxury in each of these bathrooms is the heated floors beneath the rough limestone flooring.

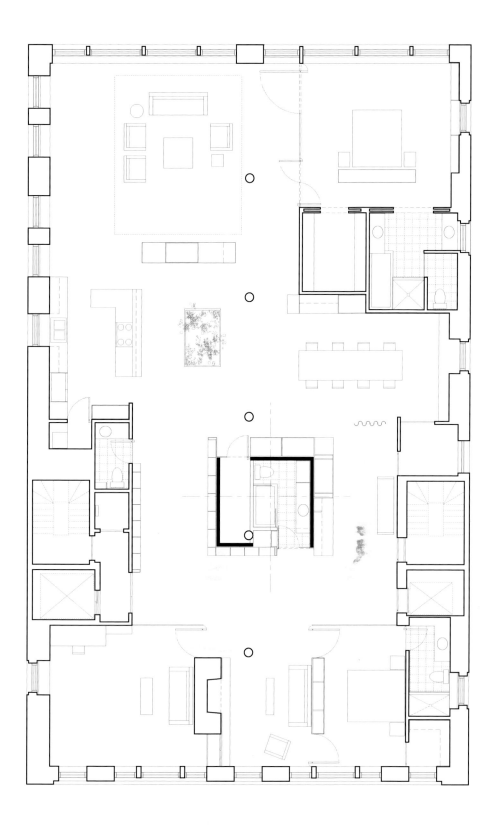

CONSTRUCTION DETAILS

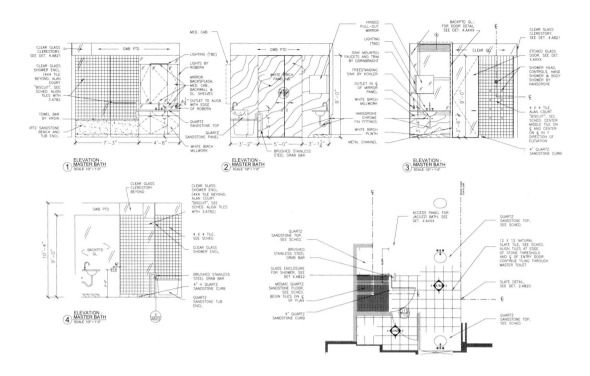

CONSTRUCTION DETAILS

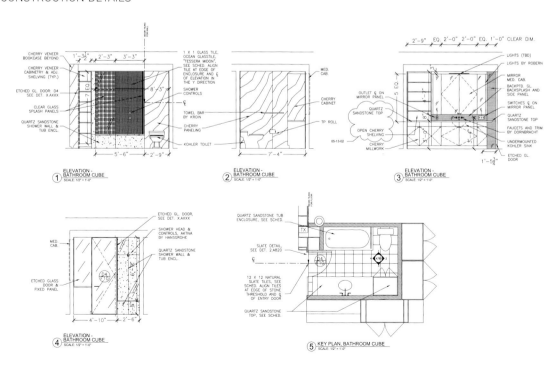

BATH WITH A VIEW

ARCHITECT HanrahanMeyers Architects

PHOTOGRAPHY Michael Moran

Wood and natural stone quarried from the site are the primary material of this contemporary house set within a natural landscape. Using this stone in the construction of walls and fireplaces, the architects were able to provide the house with an organic connection to its surroundings.

The house is intended to be experienced as a sequence of indoor and outdoor spaces. Spa areas within the house include three full baths for guest bedrooms, a powder room bath, a master bath, and the outdoor pool area, which includes an enclosed stone-lined whirlpool bath within the pool and an outdoor shower.

The master bath features a sunken tub with floor-to-ceiling windows that look out onto a twenty-five-acre wooded area. This view also looks toward a restored farmer's stone wall that the owner rebuilt as part of the landscape program for the house. Pebbles used for the shower floor reference this wall. To one side of the master bathroom, a connecting maple panel allows a visual connection to the adjacent master bedroom. A glass wall adjacent to the exterior wall includes operable casement windows to facilitate ventilation and to give a sense of connection between the bath and the wooded area it faces.

The pool is lined with local bluestone and features an inset stone-lined whirlpool bath. The poolhouse incorporates an outdoor changing room and shower. The master bath, pool, and poolhouse create areas of the compound where living spaces connect to their site.

PRINCIPAL MATERIALS PALETTE
- GREEN VERMONT MARBLE
- CLEAR GLASS
- BLUESTONE
- MAPLE
- RIVER PEBBLES

PREVIOUS PAGES: The master bath overlooks an expansive woodland. RIGHT: An inviting warm bath offers cozy, luxurious comfort on a chilly winter day.

FOLLOWING PAGES: Clear glass shower walls keep the space open and bright. The floor is covered with pebbles that reference an exterior stone wall.

BLURRING THE LINE

ARCHITECT Hanrahan and Meyers Architects

PHOTOGRAPHY Peter Aaron/ESTO Photographics

This bath is within a 1200-square-foot cedar-clad poolhouse, adjacent to an outdoor deck and pool. The house includes a new master bedroom wing with a dressing room and large master bathroom. Using a rich palette of materials that include variegated slate on the floor, handmade tiles on the walls, river stones on the floor of the shower, custom wood cabinetry, and mirror and glass surfaces, the architects attempted to bring a sense of the outdoors into the new space.

A window overlooks the surrounding wooded area, ventilating the bathroom while bringing natural light into the bath. The tub is a custom hand-hammered stainless steel whirlpool bath. The bathroom cabinetry has a hand-distressed finish with white painted wood. A steam shower has a natural stone floor, and the slate floor is heated.

Doors lead from the bedroom to a new cedar deck with an outdoor whirlpool bath. To the other side of the new master bedroom suite is a new rock garden.

The design intent was to bring a sense of nature into the bath, linking the bath to the new exterior including the gardens, rocks, water, and wooden deck.

PRINCIPAL MATERIALS PALETTE

- VARIEGATED SLATE
- HAND MADE CERAMIC TILE
- STAINLESS STEEL
- CEDAR
- RIVER STONES

FLOOR PLAN

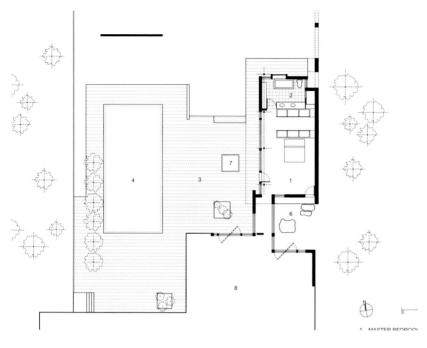

PREVIOUS PAGES: The custom
fabricated stainless steel tub is
visible in the foreground of this
spacious bathroom.
BELOW: The new addition
embraces the landscape
(Photo by Thomas Hanrahan.
RIGHT: A detail of the river stones
on the floor of the shower.

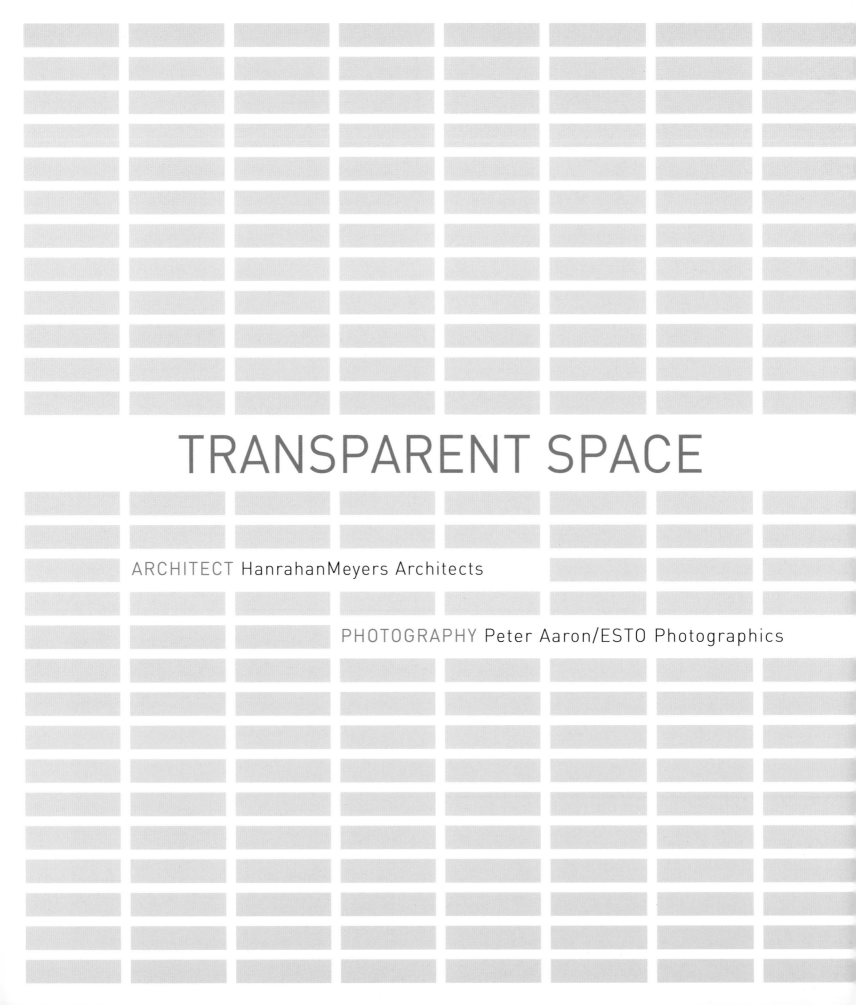

TRANSPARENT SPACE

ARCHITECT HanrahanMeyers Architects

PHOTOGRAPHY Peter Aaron/ESTO Photographics

This large loft with thirteen-foot ceilings was designed for a single person who wanted maximum transparency and openness and the ability to create private spaces when guests are visiting. The loft has two bathrooms, a guest bath tucked behind a curving translucent glass wall adjacent to the kitchen, and a large, open master bath.

This bath is designed with a clear glass enclosure that separates it from the master bedroom and dressing areas. The bath is equipped a whirlpool bath by Americh and custom steel towel bars by Scott Enge. A custom steel curtain wall enclosure with sand-blasted glass separates the bath from the living areas. Polished brown Emperador marble is used for the vanity along with maple for all of the cabinetry. The bathroom floors are covered with limestone tile.

PRINCIPAL MATERIALS PALETTE
- TRANSLUCENT AND SAND-BLASTED GLASS
- MARBLE
- STAINLESS STEEL
- MAPLE
- LIMESTONE

LEFT: A 65-foot glass wall separates the master bedroom and bath from the rest of the loft. Floor-to-ceiling curtains provide privacy when necessary.

FLOOR PLAN

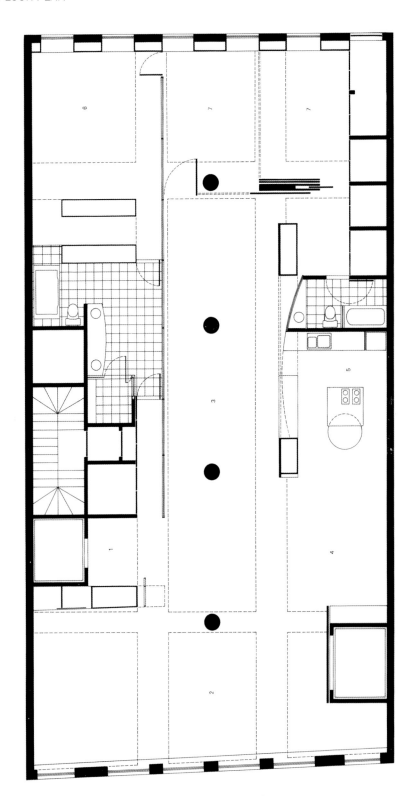

RIGHT: A view of the corridor separating the master bedroom and bathroom from the public areas of the loft.
FOLLOWING PAGES: The granite vanity with stainless steel sinks and the bath are surrounded by custom maple cabinetry.

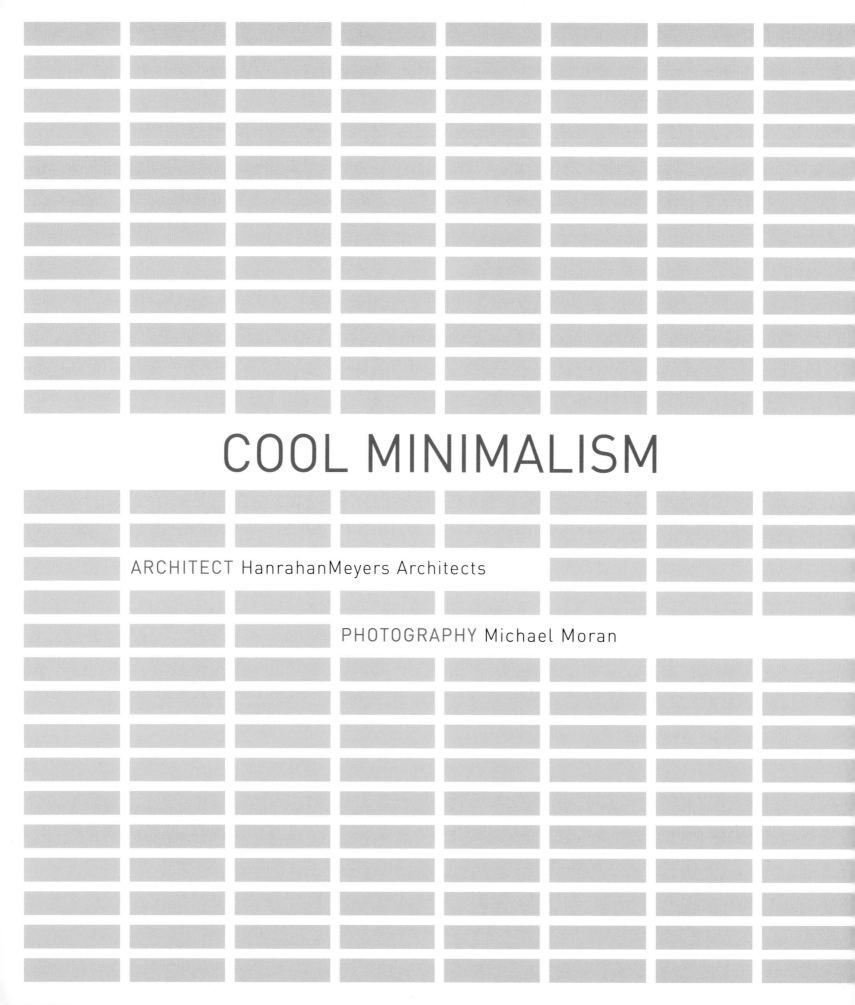

COOL MINIMALISM

ARCHITECT HanrahanMeyers Architects

PHOTOGRAPHY Michael Moran

In this minimalist Manhattan apartment, a quiet calm pervades. Ash wood is the principal material, used with different finishes for wall and door panels, shelving, and even the custom-made furniture.

Most of the ash has a white, shop-applied finish to make the apartment envelope relatively silent. Throughout the project, pieces of old ash planks with a hand-rubbed finish float within the neutral white envelope. The painted ash is acid-dipped and wire-brushed or sand-blasted, so that the wood grain appears more or less prominently. Painted panels are juxtaposed to natural-finished ash door panels and freeform ash planks from ancient trees harvested locally in upper New York State.

Ash is also used for the two bathrooms. The doors are a natural finished solid ash, and the wall panels are white-painted sand-blasted ash. In addition, translucent, handmade glass tiles are used in the shower and tub areas. They were made by MBC studios, a family-owned glass atelier in \tinue the white minimalist theme, while honed black granite is used for the counter top. One bath is separated from the living room by a wall of translucent glass. This bath has a shower. The other bath has a privacy window of painted sand-blasted ash, which can be opened to the adjacent master bedroom. The tub in this bathroom has a commanding yet soothing view of Central Park.

PRINCIPAL MATERIALS PALETTE
- SAND-BLASTED ASH PANELS
- HONED CARRARA MARBLE
- TRANSLUCENT GLASS
- HANDMADE GLASS TILES
- HONED BLACK GRANITE

LEFT: One of the two bathrooms is separated from the living area by a sand-blasted glass wall. A shower with handmade glass tiles is visible at the end of the wall.

RIGHT: The tub in the second bathroom overlooks Central Park.

FLOOR PLAN

RIGHT: An operable frosted glass
window provides a view from the
bathroom to the master bedroom
(photograph by Paul Warchol).

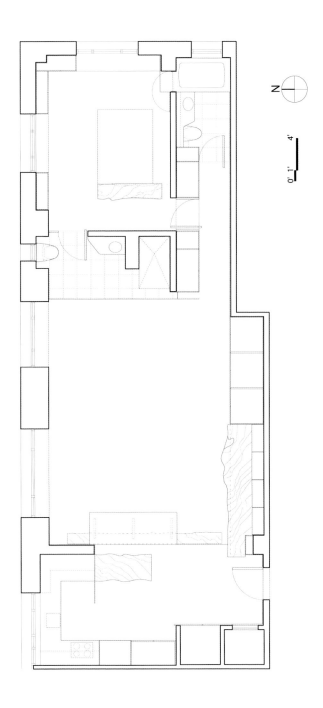

N

0' 1'   4'

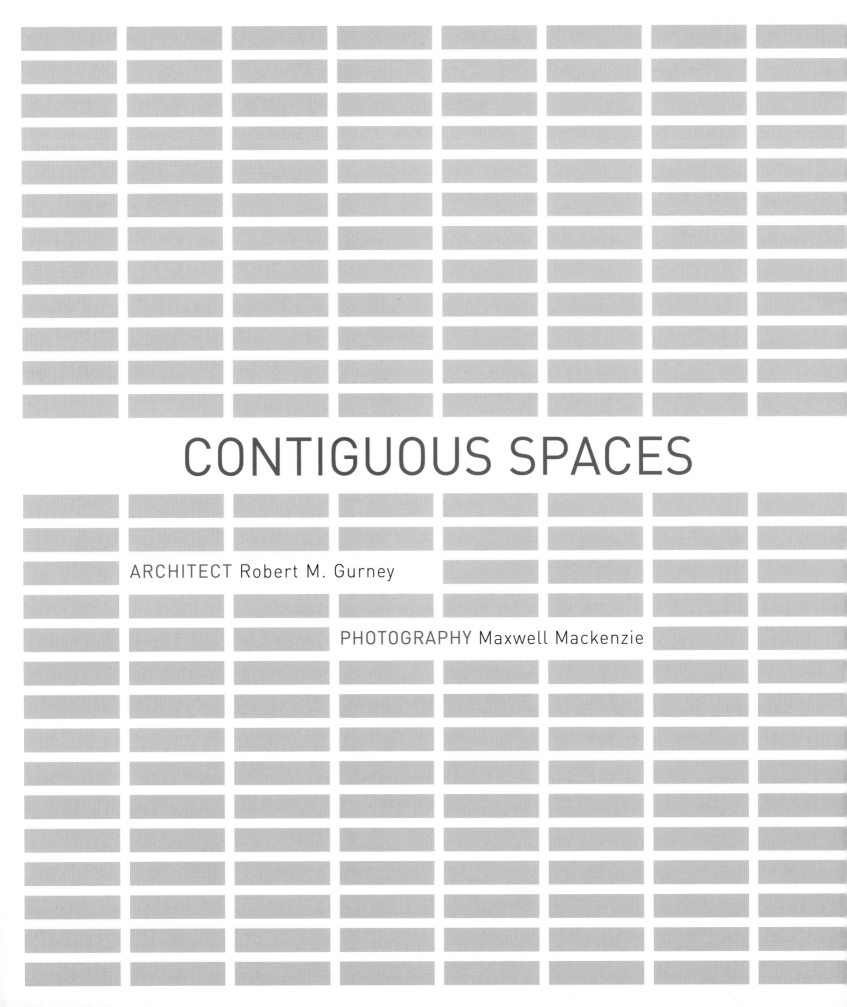

CONTIGUOUS SPACES

ARCHITECT Robert M. Gurney

PHOTOGRAPHY Maxwell Mackenzie

The goal of this bathroom renovation was to integrate a bedroom, bathroom, and closet into one contiguous space. The existing bedroom was partitioned from a large walk-in closet and a separate bathroom impeding circulation. Three interior walls were demolished to create a large open space. Then two centrally located boxlike forms were installed to serve as the focal point of the new space: a rectangular wooden bathtub was placed adjacent to a sandblasted-glass enclosed shower.

On one side of the suite, full-height wenge cabinetry stretches along an entire wall from the bedroom into the bathroom, visually and functionally binding the two spaces together. On the other side, a wenge vanity with a white marble top and stainless steel sink rests against a vertical white oak panel. Using oak and marble in the sink area as well as on the floor further unites the space visually. The vanity was placed under an existing skylight.

PRINCIPAL MATERIALS PALETTE
- WHITE MARBLE
- OAK PANELS
- SANDBLASTED GLASS
- STAINLESS STEEL
- MIRRORED GLASS
- WENGE CABINETRY

EXISTING BATHROOM FLOOR PLAN

RENOVATED BATHROOM FLOOR PLAN

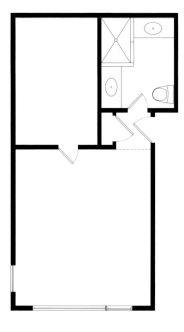

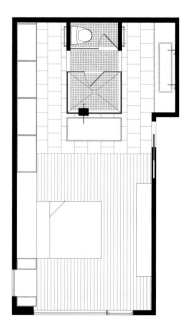

PREVIOUS PAGES: The minimalist interior is punctuated by two square forms in the center of the dressing/bath area: a rectangular wooden tub adjacent to a sandblasted-glass walk-in shower.
LEFT: A detail of the wooden tub.
RIGHT: A view of the wenge vanity with white marble top and stainless steel sinks. A vertical white oak panel serves as a contrasting backdrop.

FAR LEFT: The vanity is suspended above the white marble floor.
LEFT: An interior view of the glass-enclosed shower.
FOLLOWING PAGES: Full-height wenge cabinetry runs from the bedroom to the bathroom, functionally binding the two spaces together.

URBANE BATHROOM

ARCHITECT Robert M. Gurney

PHOTOGRAPHY Maxwell Mackenzie

Located in an 1,800-square-foot apartment in a Beaux Arts-inspired building, this bathroom reflects the minimal, urbane renovation that the client was seeking. Throughout the apartment as well as in this generously sized master bathroom, form and texture serve to unify as well as diversify spatial qualities.

Designed with formal clarity, the renovation is open and light filled, taking advantage of the apartment's corner location with windows on three sides. The door leading to the master bathroom is wenge with a frosted glass inset that allows light from the two windows in the bath to filter into the hallway. Inside, a sculptural free-standing bathtub faces a window, appearing to float above the stained oak floor. Limestone floors surround the oak flooring, and white walls, aluminum, stainless steel, translucent glass complete the minimalist pallet.

PRINCIPAL MATERIALS PALETTE
- STAINLESS STEEL
- STAINED OAK
- LIMESTONE
- WENGE
- MIRRORED GLASS

FLOOR PLAN

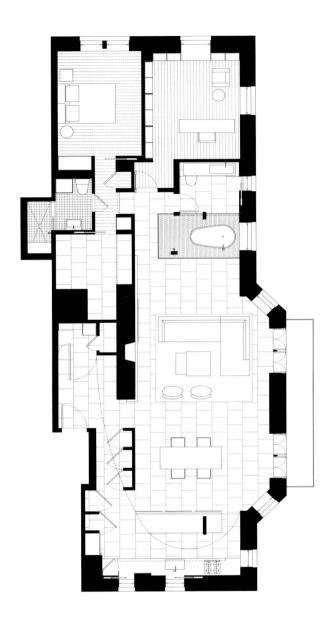

LEFT: The bathtub becomes a
sculptural object in the generously
sized bathroom.

LEFT: The wenge door frame is strongly rendered against the muted palette of limestone floors, frosted glass, and white walls.
RIGHT: The stainless steel vanity set against glass tiles, anchors the minimalist design.

RUSTIC SUSTAINABILITY

ARCHITECT Balance Associates

PHOTOGRAPHY Steve Keating

This rustic bathroom is part of a 1,400-square-foot log cabin in the Northwest designed to take advantage of passive solar heating. The construction and finish materials were selected for their sustainable qualities and are rough in texture to reflect the natural, untamed setting of the cabin. Materials for the cabin include logs, sawn beams, rough formed concrete, and corrugated metal, all of which can be found in the finish of the bathroom itself. Located on the second level of the house, the bathroom opens onto an intimate private concrete terrace that contains an outdoor shower and a free-standing stainless steel scullery sink. This area is accessed through double wood-framed glass doors.

Inside the bathroom are a rough formed concrete shower stall and a generously proportioned soaking tub. The countertop is formed from a log slab. The use of plaster walls with integral color throughout the interior of the cabin virtually eliminates the need for interior paint. Integral colored concrete gives the floor a modeled hue.

PRINCIPAL MATERIALS PALETTE
- INTEGRAL COLOR CONCRETE AND PLASTER
- ROUGH POURED CONCRETE
- RECYCLED WOOD
- STAINLESS STEEL

LEFT: A view of the bathroom through the double doors that open onto the outdoor shower.

BATHROOM PLAN

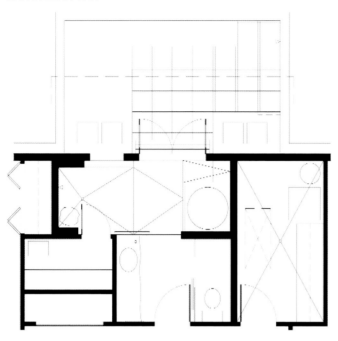

FLOOR PLAN

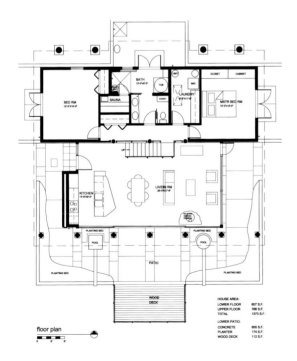

ABOVE: The entry to the sauna.
RIGHT: The outdoor shower is
tucked into the hillside. Constructed
of concrete with a stainless steel
sink, it is designed to withstand
changing weather conditions.

LEFT: The vanity top is made from a log slab.
RIGHT: A poured concrete-enclosed shower is located outside the sauna.

LEFT: An interior view showing the door leading to the outdoor shower. RIGHT: A view from the hillside of the bathroom and outdoor shower at dusk.

CLERESTORY BATHROOM

ARCHITECT Balance Associates

PHOTOGRAPHY Steve Keating

Bathrooms tend to be some of the smaller rooms in a home, so one objective is to maximize the sense of space while minimizing feelings of exposure. One way to limit the sense of exposure is to leave the toilet out of view upon entering the bathroom. In the design of this home's main bathroom, the toilet was placed on the wall adjacent to the doorway at the end of the vanity cabinet. The bathroom plan remains otherwise open without partitions separating the shower or bathing areas. Earthtone slate tiles were used for warmth and texture as well as durability. A rustic log countertop was chosen for the vanity.

A significant feature of this home is the abundance of natural lighting within. A light well from the upstairs loft provides light to this lower-level bathroom.

A compact bathroom is tucked into the upper level adjacent to a screened porch and open sleeping loft. This bathroom is more utilitarian, but takes its design cues from the main bath. Earthtone slate tile is repeated in the surrounding shower area. The tile, however, provides visual focus away from the toilet that is placed at the end of the vanity counter. The countertop angles out for extra surface area around the sink while maintaining clearance at the entry and offering an extra visual shield of the toilet upon entry. Light is offered through windows on the two outside walls of the bathroom, including one in the shower tile wall.

PRINCIPAL MATERIALS PALETTE
- SLATE
- INTEGRAL COLOR CONCRETE
- LOG SLAB
- INTEGRAL COLOR PLASTER
- MIRRORED GLASS

MASTER BATHROOM PLAN

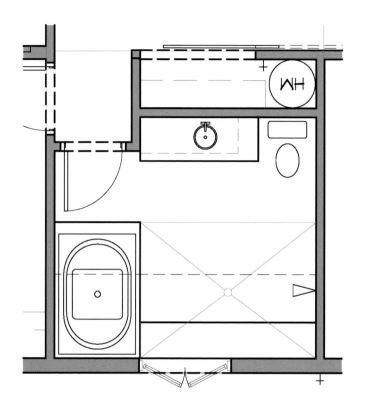

UPPER BATHROOM PLAN

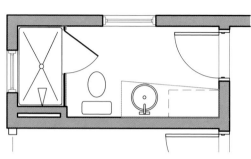

UPPER FLOOR PLAN

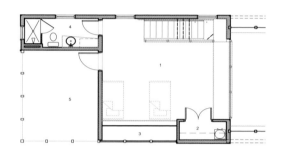

MAIN FLOOR PLAN

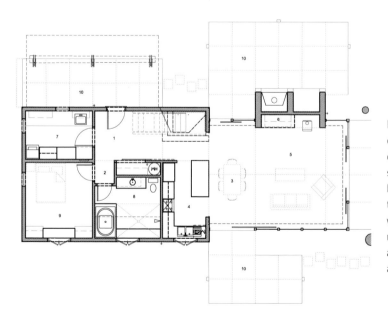

PREVIOUS PAGES: The poured concrete floor slopes gently to the open shower, making the overall space seem larger. A light well brings additional natural light into the bathroom from the clerestory windows in the loft above. The natural earthtones of the slate tile and the clear-stained pine ceiling add warmth to the bathroom.

TOP RIGHT: A detail of the light well in the main bathroom. The window is coated in polycarbonate greenhouse glazing to obscure the view from the loft above while admitting light.

RIGHT: The small upstairs bathroom, while more utilitarian, takes its design cues from the main bathroom. The toilet is obscured from immediate view thanks to the vanity countertop.

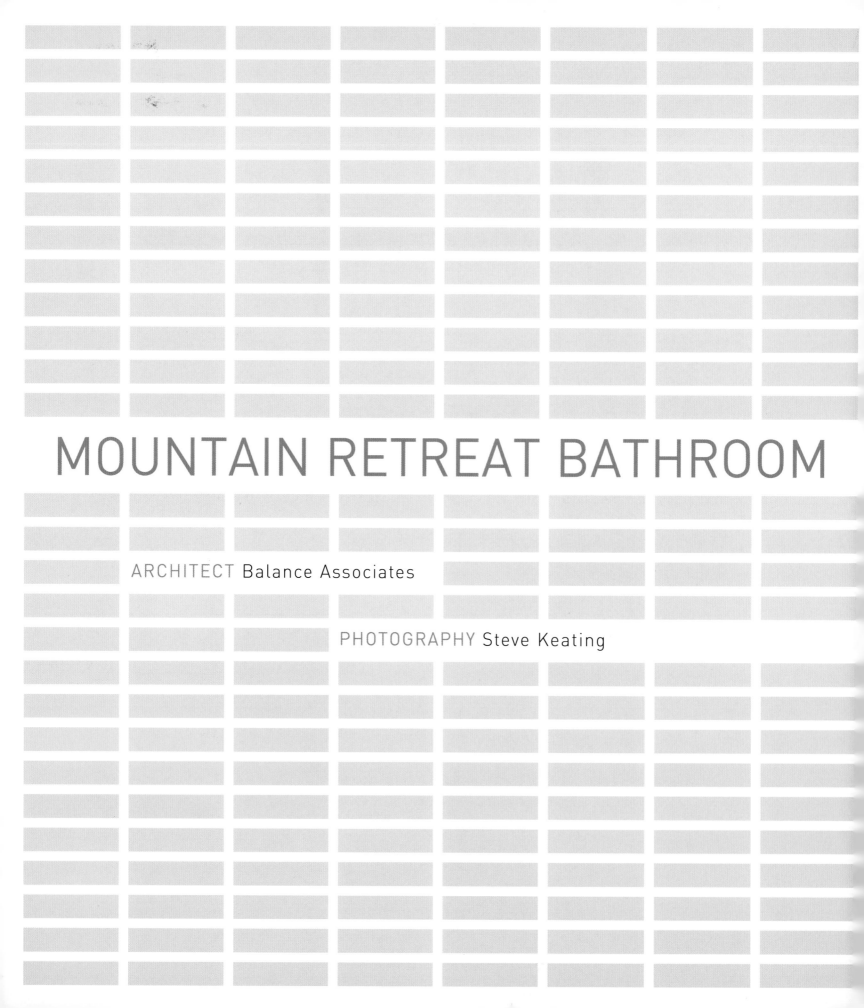

MOUNTAIN RETREAT BATHROOM

ARCHITECT Balance Associates

PHOTOGRAPHY Steve Keating

This home contains three bathrooms; a master bathroom in the master suite, a centrally located second bath, and a third bath situated between the guest suite and a workout room. Located in the corner of the upper level, the master bath is positioned to provide both privacy and views of the valley below. Both the toilet and shower compartments are contained within frosted glass partitions with surrounding windows framing mountain views. Mirrored vanity sinks provide dual linen and storage cabinets on each side of the sink counter. Integral colored concrete floors are used throughout the master suite and continue into the bathroom and shower. Custom fir cabinets with reclaimed door panels match the cabinetry used in other areas of the house. The space below the sinks is left open to extend the floor area of the room.

The second bath functions as the children's bathroom and the primary powder room. A glazed exterior door gives direct access to an outdoor shower and hot tub area. A tapered countertop provides an efficient use of space in this small bathroom. The bath counter tapers at one end, offering ample countertop space without overwhelming the scale of the small room. The counter is open below to increase the floor area of the room. An adjacent linen cabinet provides storage and also holds a laundry hamper.

PRINCIPAL MATERIALS PALETTE
- INTEGRAL COLORED CONCRETE
- RECLAIMED DOUGLAS FIR
- FROSTED GLASS
- SLATE
- MIRRORED GLASS

LEFT: The cathedral ceiling of
the master bathroom is sheathed
in reclaimed Douglas fir.
RIGHT: Sketch of the master
bathroom vanity.

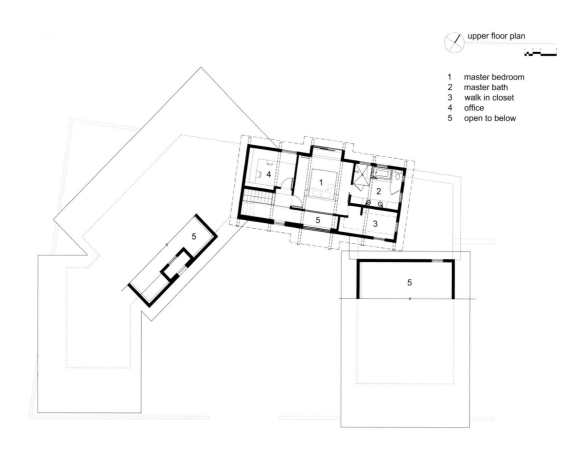

upper floor plan

1   master bedroom
2   master bath
3   walk in closet
4   office
5   open to below

RIGHT: The shower and toilet are each contained within frosted glass cubes, providing privacy as well as diffused light into these spaces. Dual linen closets are conveniently located at either end of the double-sink vanity.

FIRST FLOOR BATHROOM PLAN

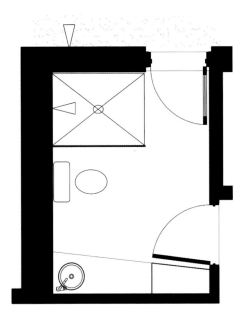

RIGHT: In the smaller first-floor bathroom, the vanity's countertop is tapered to reduce the surface area and keep the vanity in scale with the room. It is open below to reveal more floor area. The linen closet at the narrow end of the vanity offers storage.

FIRST FLOOR PLAN

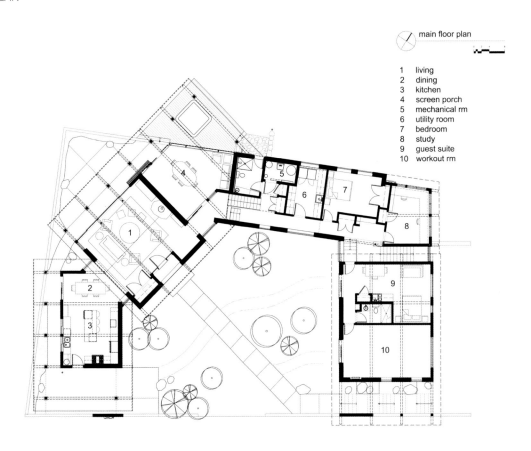

main floor plan

1 living
2 dining
3 kitchen
4 screen porch
5 mechanical rm
6 utility room
7 bedroom
8 study
9 guest suite
10 workout rm

INSIDE/OUTSIDE BATHROOM

ARCHITECT Balance Associates

PHOTOGRAPHY Steve Keating

This cabin features a master bathroom located in the master suite and a second bath that serves as both the powder room and a full bath to the other two bedrooms. Directly off the second bath is an outdoor shower located on a covered deck. The shower protrudes into an extended deck with slatted boards on two sides providing privacy while still allowing views of the surrounding countryside. Drainage valves permit easy winterization of the outdoor shower fixture.

The master bath consists of a central vanity room flanked by a large walk-in shower on one side and a toilet space on the other. A linen cabinet is situated opposite of the toilet. Sliding greenhouse polycarbonate doors provide privacy to both the toilet and showering areas. The entire bath floor is tiled in slate, which continues into the shower and up the walls. The shower pan is recessed into the shower floor eliminating a curb for a seamless transition into the shower. This allows the shower to become part of the vanity area, and creates the perception of a larger bathroom. The custom vanity was sculpted out of a large ponderosa pine with the waned edge accentuating the rustic nature of the cabin's location.

PRINCIPAL MATERIALS PALETTE

- SLATE
- KNOTTY CEDAR BOARD
- POLYCARBONATE GLAZING
- LOG SLABS
- MIRRORED GLASS

LEFT AND ABOVE: An outdoor
shower extends onto the deck of
the house. The slatted knotty
cedar boards provide a measure
of privacy without blocking views
of the valley beyond.

UPPER FLOOR PLAN

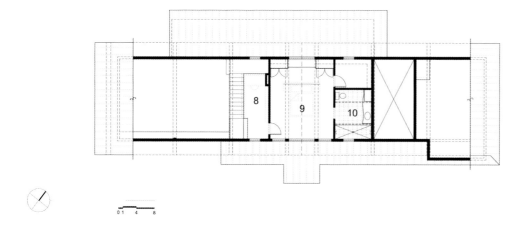

0 1 4 8

MAIN FLOOR PLAN

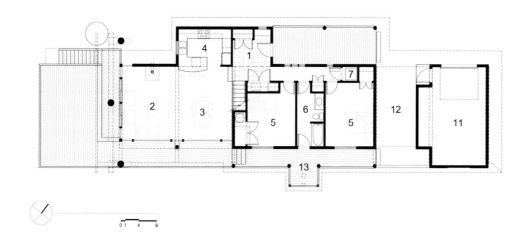

0 1 4 8

1 entry
2 living
3 dining
4 kitchen
5 bedroom
6 bath
7 laundry
8 den
9 master bedroom
10 master bath
11 garage
12 breezeway
13 outdoor shower

MAIN FLOOR BATH AND OUTDOOR SHOWER

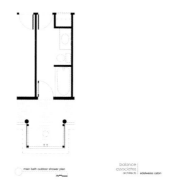

main bath outdoor shower plan

balance
associates
architects | edelweiss cabin

RIGHT: The vanity in the master bathroom is fashioned from a large ponderosa log. Slate is used for the floor, shower, and walls in one continuous gesture.

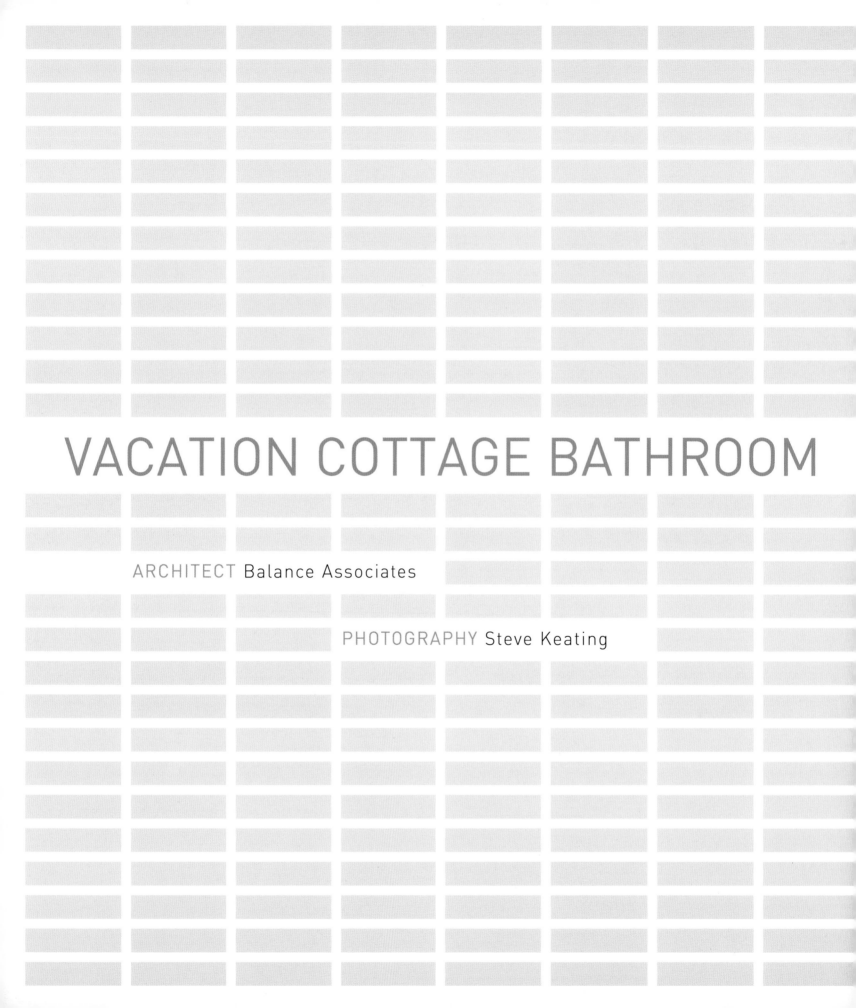

VACATION COTTAGE BATHROOM

ARCHITECT Balance Associates

PHOTOGRAPHY Steve Keating

The master bathroom in this vacation home is part of to the master suite on the upper level. The materials used in the bathroom are repeated throughout the house: custom maple cabinets, composite countertops, slate tile, and minimal stainless steel fixtures and hardware. Composite countertops of resin and paper form the vanity counter, shower bench, and shower shelf, surrounded by walls of slate tile. A clerestory window between the bath and the master bedroom serves to divide the space while allowing light from the bathroom into the bedroom. This clerestory glazing also allows the wood-slated ceiling to run continuously in both the bath and bedroom, visually increasing the size of both rooms. An integral colored concrete floor is used in the bathroom and the shower. Windows on all three exterior walls of the bathroom frame selected views.

PRINCIPAL MATERIALS PALETTE

- SLATE
- STAINLESS STEEL
- MAPLE
- INTEGRAL COLORED CONCRETE
- PAPER AND RESIN COMPOSITE COUNTERTOPS

MASTER BATH PLAN

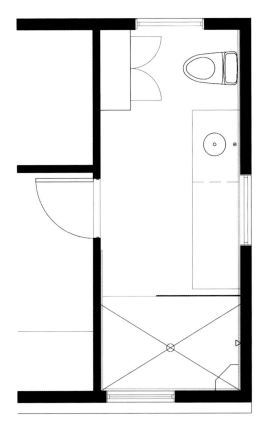

UPPER FLOOR PLAN

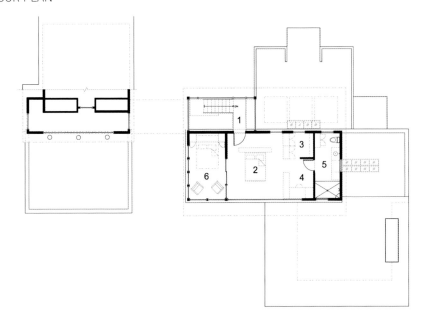

1   stair
2   master bedroom
3   walk in closet
4   study
5   bath
6   sleeping porch

ABOVE: A view from the master
bedroom past the open study
area to the master bathroom.
A clerestory window visually
divides the space while allowing
the Douglas fir ceiling to run
continuously between both spaces.

LEFT, ABOVE, AND RIGHT: The vanity's countertop is made of a composite of paper and resin. The open shower and walls are covered with slate tiles. The integrated color cement floor continues into the open shower, all contributing to a visual impression that the room is larger than it is. Windows on three sides capture dramatic views.

TWO GARDEN HOUSES

ARCHITECT Balance Associates

PHOTOGRAPHY Steve Keating

PRINCIPAL MATERIALS PALETTE
- FROSTED GLASS
- CLEAR GLASS
- MILESTONE
- STAINED CONCRETE
- BLACK SLATE
- GLASS TILES

These two houses form a single compound and are set side by side in a park like setting in a suburban neighborhood. They are arranged to take advantage of extensive gardens surrounding them.

There are two bathrooms in Garden House One, a master suite and a children's bath. The first-floor children's bathroom contains functional spaces within the bathroom that create privacy zones. Frosted glass partitions separate the toilet and bathing area from the vanity while allowing natural light throughout. A bright red milestone shower and bathtub enclosure add color to the otherwise neutral space. The stained concrete floors throughout the home are used for radiant hear. The master bathroom for Garden House One is designed along a linear path extending from the master bedroom and ending at the walk-in closet. A large central skylight above floods the room with natural light and subdivides the room into quadrant. Each quadrant is designed around a fixture—the shower, a soaking tub, the toilet, and the vanity—each connected along the central circulation path. Glass mosaic tile create a soothing background for the glass-enclosed shower stall.

In Garden House Two, the bathroom on the main floor accommodates two first-floor bedrooms. The walk-in shower, located at the back of this bathroom, is the focal point. Three shades of crimson glass mosaic tile are used from floor to ceiling to create a rich and lively surface. Upstairs, the master bathroom is designed as an extension of the master suite. The bedroom, walk-in closet, and bathroom spaces are unified by an an open vaulted ceiling with exposed curved wood Glue-Lam beams and steel tie rods. A skylight along the peak of the vault illuminates the entire suite. Spaces within the suite are divided with wood cabinetry, and can be closed off using sliding partitions. In the center of the bathroom is a freestanding walk-in shower. The wall and floor of the shower are constructed from a single-cleft black slate slab. The soaking tub and cantilevered vanity are located on the perimeter of the bathroom, anchoring the space.

LEFT: In Garden House One, the master bathroom enjoys natural light from a skylight running the length of the space. A generous glass enclosed walk-in shower is the focal point of the bathroom.

GARDEN HOUSE ONE BATHROOM PLAN

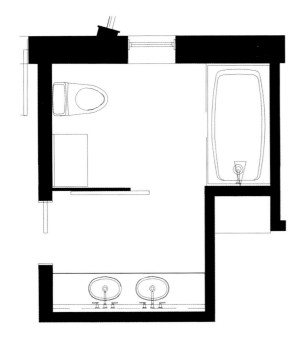

GARDEN HOUSE ONE MASTER BATHROOM PLAN

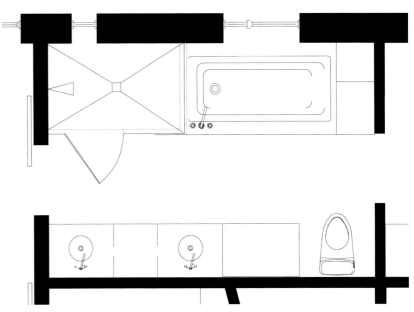

GARDEN HOUSE ONE & TWO MAIN FLOOR PLAN

main floor plan

1   entry
2   hall
3   courtyard
4   bedroom
5   play room
6   vanity
7   bath
8   laundry
9   kitchen/dining
10 living
11 patio
12 master suite
13 office
14 mechanical
15 garage
16 rain garden

LEFT AND RIGHT: In the main bathroom of Garden House One, the toilet and tub area can be separated from the vanity area by sliding frosted glass panels. When closed, these panels allow light from the window into the vanity area.

GARDEN HOUSE TWO BATHROOM PLAN

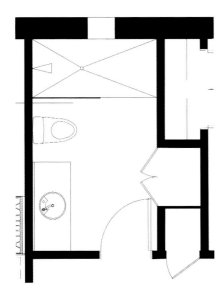

GARDEN HOUSE TWO MASTER BATHROOM PLAN

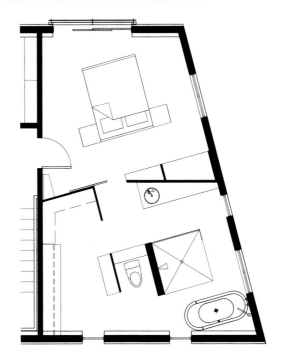

LEFT: In the main bathroom of
Garden House Two, three shades
of crimson glass tile enliven the
bathing area.

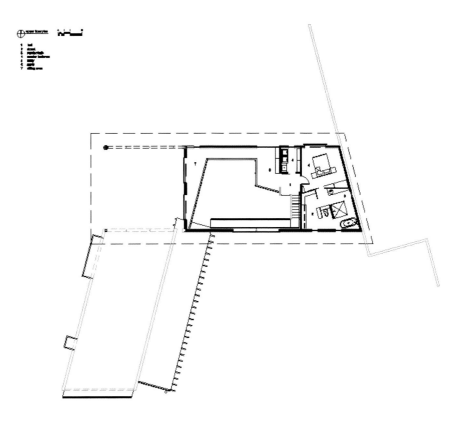

LEFT: The bathroom and bedroom in the second floor master suite of Garden House Two are unified by an open vaulted ceiling. The dressing/bath area is separated from the bedroom with bookcases and sliding wood panels.

RIGHT: The large bathroom has an open shower with an enclosed toilet tucked behind.

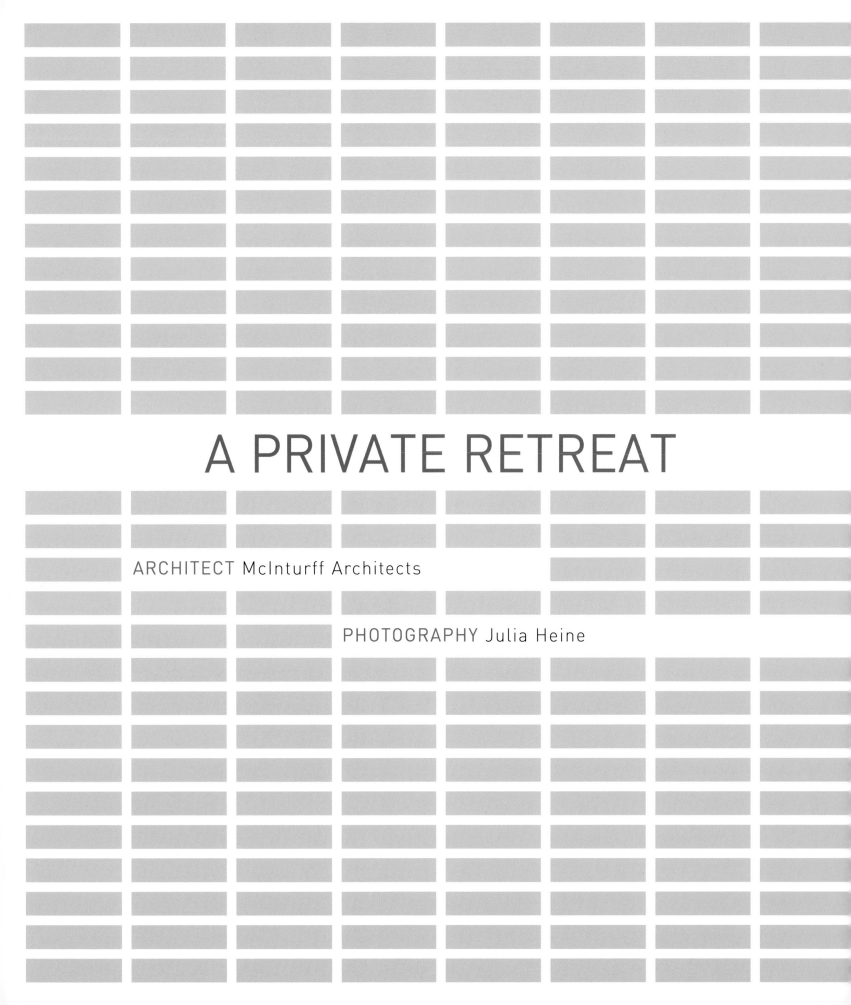

A PRIVATE RETREAT

ARCHITECT McInturff Architects

PHOTOGRAPHY Julia Heine

The architects designed this master suite for a client with whom they had worked over a period of years, renovating various areas of the house. This was the last addition—a private retreat that includes a bedroom and a generous open bath and dressing area on the main level, with a meditation room above. A gym and storage area complete the lower level. Furniture, all designed by the architect, was kept to a minimum.

The bathroom itself was designed around a 3,000-pound limestone bathtub cut from a single block of stone. It is thrust into nature, surrounded by a glass-enclosed atrium.

A wooden tower, placed within the simple white brick gable of the addition, rises up through the roof. It houses the meditation, dressing, and massage spaces. The exceptional wood detailing of the tower and of the stair that connects the three levels was the work of a master carpenter with whom the architect has worked in the past. ·

PRINCIPAL MATERIALS PALETTE

- STATUARY MARBLE
- MAHOGANY PANELS
- HONED NERO MARQUINA SLAB
- POLISHED NICKEL
- MIRRORED GLASS

SECTION

PREVIOUS PAGES: The custom
limestone tub is reflected in the
mirror above the limestone vanities.
RIGHT: Simple geometric forms
define the master bedroom/bathroom
addition. The tower floating above the
bathroom contains a meditation space.

BATHROOM PLAN

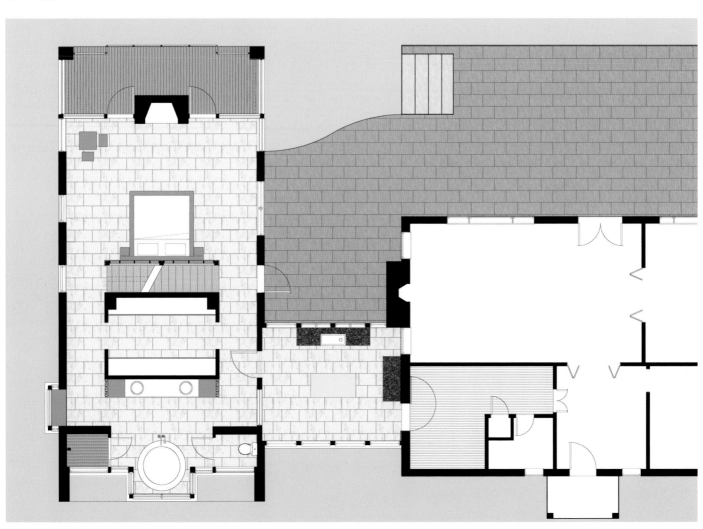

LEFT: From the bathtub, one can enjoy the seclusion of its natural setting. A walk-in shower is adjacent.

ABOVE: In the master bedroom addition, a fireplace is positioned at the end of the bed, and surrounded by glass.

LEFT AND RIGHT: Fine craftsmanship is evident in the constrution of the natural fir wooden tower that contains the staircase connecting the upper and lower levels and separating the master bedroom from the master bathroom.

FOLLOWING PAGES: A view into the master bedroom from the snow-covered exterior.

A GLASS BATHROOM

ARCHITECT McInturff Architects

PHOTOGRAPHY Julia Heine

This bathroom was designed for European clients living in the United States. They wanted the architects to reverse the typical American master bedroom/bathroom layout in their existing house by moving the bedroom into the former bath/dressing room and dedicating the larger existing bedroom space to a combined bath and dressing area. In response, the architects created a glass bathing chamber, including sinks, tub, and shower, as a free-standing structure within a larger dressing and closet area. All of the surfaces—doors, walls, tub surround, and vanity countertops—are clad in glass to allow light to create a shimmering environment for this space during the day and at night.

PRINCIPAL MATERIALS PALETTE

- CLEAR GLASS
- BACK-PAINTED GLASS
- MIRRORED GLASS
- GLASS TILE

SECTION

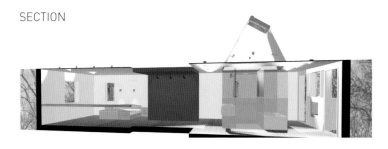

PREVIOUS PAGES: A view from
the master bedroom to the
glass-enclosed bathroom module
in the dressing area, formerly the
master bedroom.
RIGHT: A model of the glass-
enclosed bathroom area.
RIGHT: Glass door detail.

EXISTING BATHROOM PLAN

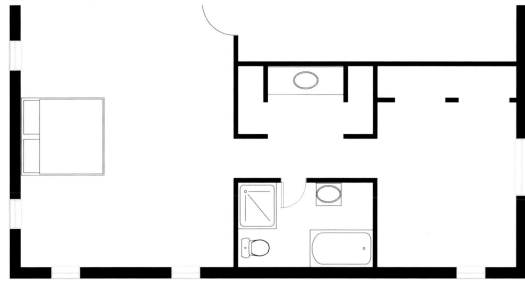

RENOVATED BATHROOM PLAN

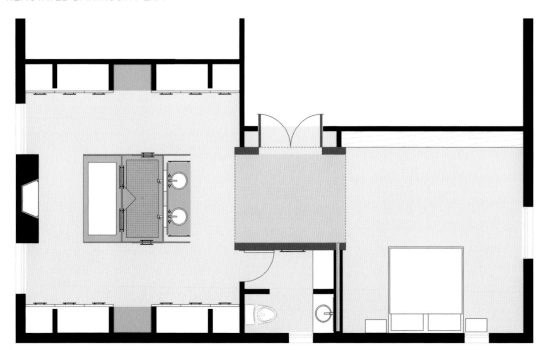

LEFT: Dual showers are sandwiched between the bathtub and the vanity, all surrounded by glass.

ABOVE: The glass bath module floats within the larger dressing area with windows on three sides.

LEFT: The tub is encased in back-painted glass.
ABOVE: The countertops for the vanity are also back-painted glass.

MALIBU MINIMALISM

ARCHITECT Kanner Architects

PHOTOGRAPHY John Linden

In order to incorporate some aspects of Japanese bathing rituals, the owner and the architect toured small hotels in Japan for inspiration. The resulting bathroom reflects the Japanese minimalism they encountered. The house itself is inspired by Luis Barragan, the Mexican architect who is considered a master of space and light and is known for his sculptural courtyard designs. The 3,200-square-foot building is anchored by a serene interior court that serves as the entry to the house. Operable glass walls fold and slide to open the house to the outside, removing barriers between residents and horizon and leaving unobstructed views of mountains and ocean. The home was designed to take full advantage of its secluded location and the breathtaking views on a crest in the Malibu Hills. The exterior white plaster walls are a sharp counterpoint to the blue sky and the Pacific Ocean. Inside, the warm mahogany floors, doors, and cabinets offer a welcoming contrast. The home's plan establishes a hierarchy of space through varying ceiling heights. Vertical space is greatest in the living room, dining room, and master bedroom.

Japanese-inspired touches in the bathroom include a large soaking tub, or *ofuro*, and a separate compartment for the toilet, complete with a clerestory window. There is also a separate area for bathing Japanese-style while sitting on a low stool. The large glass-enclosed shower overlooks the swimming pool.

PRINCIPAL MATERIALS PALETTE
- LIMESTONE SLABE
- BLACK-HONED GRANITE
- DOUGLAS FIR
- MIRRORED GLASS

BATHROOM PLAN

PREVIOUS PAGES AND RIGHT: The master bathroom opens onto the swimming pool area, creating the sense of being in a private resort. FOLLOWING PAGES: The bathroom is finished in vertical-grained Douglas fir and white limestone.

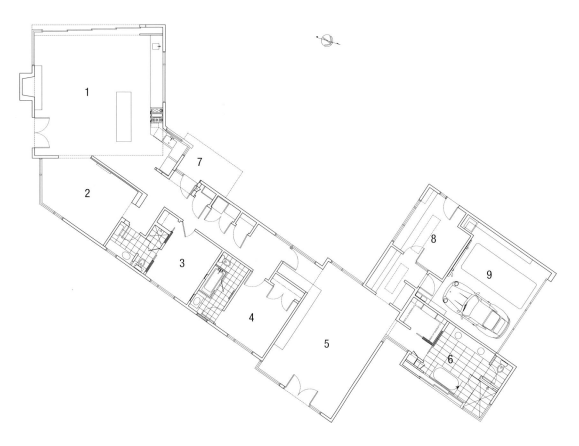

1. Living room, dining room, kitchen
2. Den
3. Bedroom
4. Bedroom
5. Master bedroom
6. Master bathroom
7. Entry
8. Home office
9. Garage